IMPRESSIONS OF WARRIORS AND CLOWNS

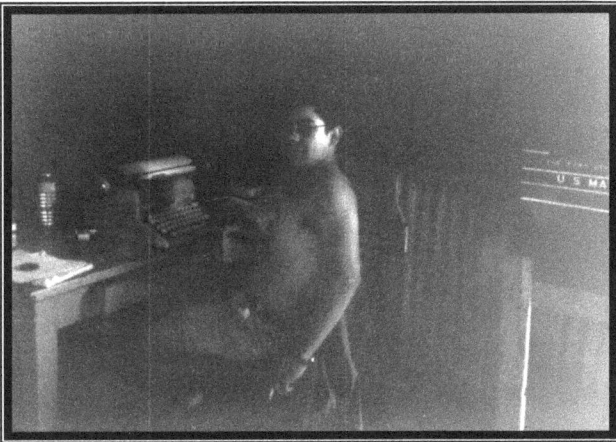

Author on Lowja Island
Enewetak Atoll, Marshall Islands
Nuclear Clean-up Project
1977-1978

Impressions

of

Warriors

and

Clowns

by

Julio V. Sosa Jr.

2nd Edition

Printed at Akron, Ohio

IMPRESSIONS OF WARRIORS AND CLOWNS

ISBN: 0-9821567-0-7

PUBLISHED BY JULIO V. SOSA
www.sosa-publishing.com
San Francisco

Printed in the United States of America

Dedicated to

Those Who Serve
Past, Present and Future

The Cadets of Lowell High School Junior ROTC
and
The San Francisco Junior ROTC Program
1916 – Beyond

The Military Family

IN MEMORIAM

Mom and Dad

CONTENTS

*Every man has a right to risk his own life
in order to preserve it.*
                    -ROUSSEAU-

AUTHOR'S NOTE

This is the second edition of "Impressions of Warriors and Clowns." In this edition I have added three previously unpublished poems, one of which is my first attempt in writing in Spanish. The Spanish poem is called Pasión, which translates to Passion, and was written in 1989, the English translation is included. I have also added "Día De Los Muertos" which translates to "Day of the Dead," also written in 1989. The third poem is "Steel Pot" written in 2005.

I first started writing poetry as a way to learn English, as it is my second language. However, my Spanish was stifled during my elementary years as a means to have me learn English. Adding dyslexia to the equation I had a very difficult time trying to express myself. Luckily for me I found a teacher who taught me or let me say gave me a gift of poetry. So if my sentence is incomplete or punctuation is out of place ... I claim poetic license and offer my sincere apology.

The inception of "Impressions of Warriors and Clowns," was during my high school years and during the height of the Vietnam War, dark days for our Nation and many a high school student. It was a time of uncertainties – the draft, civil unrest and the oil embargo. I found refuge in the bowels of Lowell High School, better known as "RO" (Junior ROTC). I am forever grateful to my JROTC instructors, Sergeant Majors Thomas Callahan and Mack Yoshida, for persuading me to stay in school and putting my military career on hold until I graduated.

Spending ten years on active duty with the U.S. Army, I continued to write and added to the collection. The book was brought to fruition a few months after being honorably discharged. Although some of the poems are dark, this book is about redemption, love and life. There is no shame in love for one's country, nor dishonor in serving her. This book is for the soldier, the warrior, and that clown in all of us.

Our Country finds itself at war and many warriors have made the ultimate sacrifice. Others find themselves battling inner demons. If you or a love one seems to be suffering from depression, mental health issues or posttraumatic stress disorder (PTSD) seek help immediately. If you believe it is an emergency dial 911. On the following page I have include a list of resource and contact information. By no means is this list inclusive, and other resources may be available in your community.

The Author

The National Suicide Prevention Lifeline: A 24-hour, toll-free suicide prevention service available to anyone in suicidal crisis. If you need help, please dial 1-800-273-TALK (8255). **Veterans** can dial 1-800-273-TALK (8255) and press 1 to connect to VA suicide prevention and mental health service professionals.

Military OneSource is provided by the Department of Defense at no cost to active duty, Guard and Reserve (regardless of activation status) and their families. It is a virtual extension of installation services. Visit www.militaryonesource.com or call 1-800-342-9647.

Department of Veterans Affairs: 1-800-827-1000.
If you are experiencing a medical emergency or in need of immediate crisis counseling, please go to your nearest medical facility Emergency Room or call 911. If you are in need of immediate crisis counseling, please contact VA's suicide hotline at 1-800-273-TALK; counselors are available 24/7 to help.

American Red Cross: Disaster Services & Emergency Assistance to find a shelter, obtain emergency food, water and other disaster relief, contact your local Red Cross chapter or call 1-800-REDCROSS (1-800-733-2767) or 1-800-257-7575 (Español).

There are many agencies and organizations ready to help. Please check your local directory for contact information.

Impressions of Warriors and Clowns

Impressions of Warriors and Clowns
both shed tears
both have hearts.

The warriors' scars show not the
Loneliness or sorrow of lost Love.
He's callous to showing of emotions, but no matter
he feels.

Clowns hide behind make-up, floppy shoes
and baggy pants.   A smile which truly
is a frown.   He doesn't show it, but he feels.

Impressions of Warriors and Clowns
both shed tears
both have hearts.

The Pray

Father you have given
me strength in my hour
of weakness.

Faith in my hour
of despair.

Hope when life seemed
hopeless.

Love where there
was hate.

Prisoner

I live suspended in time
thinking of you.

A sentence in the war of love
captured by your beauty.

The Call

Midnight call
sad awakening
howling wind, crying sky
a friend has died.

John William

Tear drops fell from the sky
the night I heard John William died.

An empty glass an empty stool
where he once sat.

A rosary and good memories
I'll always keep with me.

One last toast farewell my friend
I'll miss you by my side.

Fantasy

The moon overhead
I see you in my bed
in a fantasy of my mind.

A ship in the night
the sail all white
I see your face
in the crashing waves.

Flying through the air
I feel your long hair
upon my sweating body.

The earth beneath me
shall you not touch
for you are the virgin
of my dreams.

Marriage

I feel my skin
upon yours and
yours beneath mine.

The love which we
have made
uniting us in one.

Blessed by God
through the eyes
of men.

Bind together for
all men to see on the
Altar of the Church.

WIFE

Remembrance of times gone by,
the love I knew, your faithfulness,
truthfulness, guidance,
a friend, lover,
my wife

Rumors

Rumors past and
life goes by
no one remembers
where they started.

People hurt from
malicious gossip
when will they stop.

A man knows who he is
and what he is,
God the only judge.

Yesterday

We were young yesterday
a day younger.

Now we grow older
with the days passing.

Feel each minute each hour as it passes
for it's our lives going by.

Don Quixote

Lost in my world of books,
a land of mystery.

Cervantes', Don Quixote
living in dreams.

Where is Sancho,
my Lady Dulcinea?

Windmills and dragons
upon my lance.

Of death and life
I am sure, but of Love I am not.

Totality

Lovers searching
for one, hoping that
one day a life will be complete.

Patience

Life a seed
it grows with time
Just like love.

We fly in space
in an incredible rate
But life and love take time.

Searching

Living two lives
within one soul.
Searching for love
someone to hold.
In a life full of joy and
sorrow.
A goal a reason
for tomorrow.

Memories

My life goes on although you are gone,
but memories of you linger on.

Your firm white breast, morsels to
refresh my love hungry soul no longer
will I digest.

No longer will I flavor your rose
petal lips upon my taste buds.

Your soft long hair will no longer
veil unblemished body which
once was mine.

Time has taken you my love, but time
must go on that others may love as we.

Time

Love a time in the day to want
or a time of yesterday?
What can we make of love,
who is to say of my love?
Only you can say
for you are what makes me love
and that is all I care about.

The Lake

The grey lake calm and still
the reeds tall and greenish brown.

The laughter of ducks
from nature's shelter.

Singing birds from
within the trees.

Barriers

Love, no barriers,
man does not choose.
The heart, the eyes decide.

Life

Life a beginning to an end
Time for wanting and for loving
Sharing until eternity, happiness, sadness.
Life and death.

Leaving You

Hollowness within my soul
a love story to be told.
Traveling to other lands,
leaving you in someone else's hands,
I should have let things be.
I would be happier and I'd be me.

Eternity

Living, loving, wanting to be
in love with you for eternity.

Give me a kiss, give me a hug
tell me how much it is you love.

Tell me yes and it will be done
soon you will know the meaning of love.

Deployment

The warmth of your body
on a cold night.
A refreshing kiss
for my thirst.

A soothing touch
for my aching heart.
This is what I'll miss.

I'm leaving on a long trip
lonely and afraid,
hoping that I'll make
it home to live another day.

For now good-bye, I cannot stay
I'm off to fight for you
so that I may live at home with you
in peace and unafraid.

Home

TV's on
Radio blasting

Coffee boiling
Toast popping

Water running
Children crying

I love it
It's home

Monday

Rattling of tires
honking horns.

Shrieking sirens
shutting doors.

Work week beginning
a routine in life.

San Francisco

Mystic City,
Magic nights.
Golden Gate
on the Bay,
engulfing me in her spell.

Son

An infant in my arms
fast asleep.
My child, your son
our mingled blood.

Conceived in love
when we became one.

May love remain with him
throughout the days,
so he may love as we
have done, when we became one.

Betrayed

You betrayed heart and soul
for a few coins of gold.
Now I find myself alone
emptiness within.
Drinking wine to forget
the sorrow I have known.

Street Lights

The artificial light in the night
stars covered by clouds.

Children laughing and looking high
acting older than they really are.

An artificial high is not for me
I love life as it is.

I've tasted wine I've smelled the smoke,
But it's not really me.

Judas

Kiss of Judas or of love
which is it that you give?

Do you love or despise
is your love disguised?

Tell me love is true.
Or have I just been a fool?

Tomorrow

A child born in innocence
as my love for you.

With a new son
is born a new day.

Let's forget yesterday
and live for tomorrow.

Darkness

I reached into darkness
to see if you were there
I smelled, touched, listened
I looked everywhere.

Where are you my love
where are you my dear
I feel the ache, the pain
of knowing you are near.

I hunger to touch your
long black hair
your ruby lips
your melon breast.

I know I need you
like the fish the sea
birds the sky
earth the seed.

We loved before
We shall love again
But never the same
twice in a day.

Suicidal Ideation

One last drink before I go,
as I sit on my velvet throne.
One last drop to wash the ill
as I pop this magic pill.
No more pain, no more trouble
as I take this final bow.
The grand finale as I choose
my own demise.

Suicide

Lost in a whirlpool
of sorrow
No where to turn
only a bottle.

Pills, booze
way to end it.
Razor slice of flesh
death.

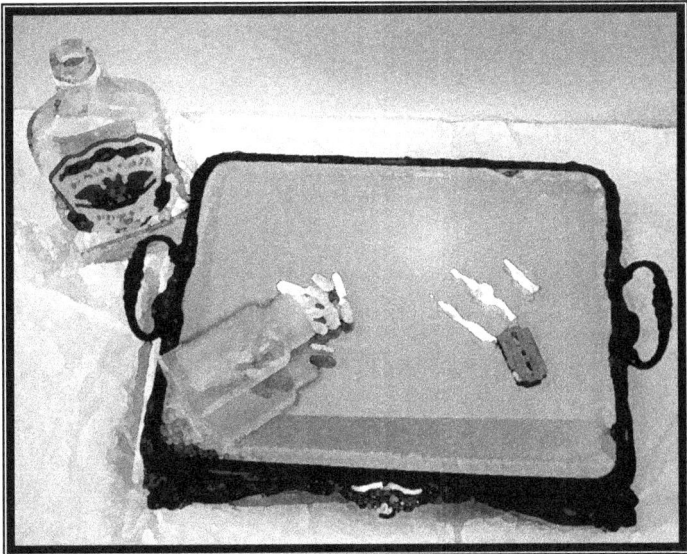

Promise Land

Son today you become
a man.   I left our
family in your hands.

God called me away today
I'm bound to the promised land.

Don't be afraid of my
journey for I follow
the Shepherd and His staff.

Kiss

A kiss
your lips
A desire I won't miss.

The highest mountain
the deepest sea
wouldn't hold me back
from the love I have for you.

Emptiness

Time has stopped
since you left
I now feel emptiness.

I never told you how much
I loved you, how much
you meant to me.

Now you are gone
and I am alone
until eternity.

Word

The rains wash away
the soil as my tears
wash away memories of you.

Only one kind word
would have sufficed,
but love I never heard.

I never said it.
I never could.
For I was a fool.

Journey

I took a voyage to another
world.
A journey to the unknown,
to find a love I thought
I'd miss, to discover
Love was gone.

War

I sit contemplating on
my past as I watch life
pass me by.   Death and misery
in a world full of uncertainties.

No where to turn
No where to go.

Wars fought for God
and principles, no one wins, all
are losers in a world
full of hate.

No where to turn
No where to go.

Time passes
No one learns
Cycle repeating
No end
Death.

Sorrow

Forgetting the time
which has passed
for sorrow it brings.

Love lost never
to be regained,
for you have gone.

Voyage

Never ending voyage
through the passage of time
searching, searching for
a love of mine.

Hopelessly lost in a
whirlpool of lust
searching, searching for
an endless love.

Tomorrow might bring
happiness, but today I am sad
searching, searching for
a love of mine.

Flight Home

Waiting
for the flight home.
Waiting to hold
you in my arms.

Waiting
for your warm embrace
waiting to kiss
your lovely face.

Duty calls and
off I'll go again,
Waiting
for the flight home.

Corpsman

Explosions all around
hit the dirt for cover
plead to God for one more day.

Incoming you hear
cries for corpsman
smell of sulfur in the air.

Ringing in your ears
fighting subsides
it's over at least for now.

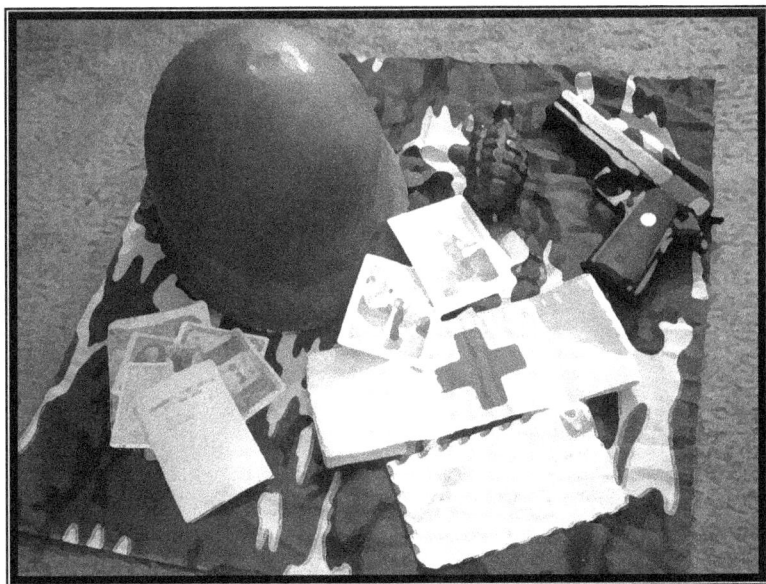

Smoke Covered Valley

Smoke covered valley Swiss cheese
terrain.

What are we fighting for
what are we to gain?

Bullets flying through the air
you stop, look, listen everywhere.

Turn to a spot and there he lies
your best buddy as he dies.

Tear drops fall from your eyes
then you realize men can cry too.

Fallen Warriors

Crimson river
Valley of Death
Fallen Warriors
lie where they died
An unknown war
on foreign soil
As we reap the spoils

Flames of Freedom

A cry of a child
piercing the night.
A stillness in
the air.
Flames of freedom in the
distance.
Hunger everywhere.
Heroes made cowards die.
Simple lies taking lives.
Why?

Tears

We fought and died for peoples lives.
For children and mothers with tears in their eyes.

So Freedom might ring around the land
we left our dead in Vietnam.

The Steel Pot

The steel pot was a friend of mine
from Word War II to Vietnam
I shaved my face and brushed my teeth
and many of times soaked my feet

Cooked my meals
dug some holes
boiled coffee
washed my clothes

'til this day
I owe a lot
to this amazing steel pot.

Día De Los Muertos
Day Of The Dead

The flowers die, but
they bloom again, a yearly ritual
of renewal.

We laugh at death, at least on this day.
Laughter hides our sadness, our fear of death,
like the mask that cover our faces.

Altars adorn with familiar symbols of the life
our love ones led. They have not left us, but
live in our memories.

We flirt with death, as a young girl
will with boys, only to say no to the
invitations.

Candles flicker, illuminating the darkness, as
those who we celebrate illuminated our dark
lives.

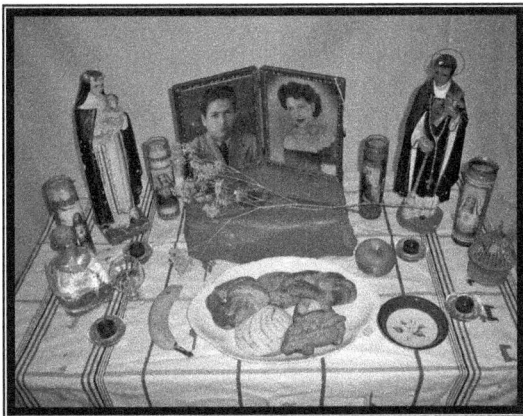

Pasión

La Pasión De
Amor, Odio Y Honor
Como Un Espíritu En La
Oscuridad Esperando
Su momento para aparecer

Que Fantasma Eres Tú
Pasión Huyendo Esta
Juventud Que No Te Ha
Conocido

Despierte Aquella Alma
Que Parece Fallecida
Prendes La Llama
De El Tiempo Pasado
Para Iluminar El Camino
De Nuestro Destino

Passion

The Passion Of
Love, Hate, and Honor
Like A Spirit in the Darkness
Seeking its Moment to Appear

What Type of Phantom Are You
Passion Eluding This Generation
Which has not known you

Awaken These Souls
Which Appear Dead
Lighting the Flames
Of Those Days Gone By
Illuminating the Path
To Our Destiny

www.ingramcontent.com/pod-product-compliance
Lightning Source LLC
Chambersburg PA
CBHW070109070426
42448CB00038B/2389